Original publication: "Notopísanka 1"
Author: Eva Šašinková, M.M., Ph.D., M.B.A.
Illustrations: Mgr. Kateřina Kovářová
Original graphic design: Lumír Kaděra
Original publisher: Czech Music Edition, Prague, Czech Republic, 2022
Website: www.hudebni-publikace.cz
Copyright: Eva Šašinková, M.M., Ph.D., M.B.A.
Original Czech version ISBN: 978-80-908169-8-5

English adaptation: "Clefi's Music Workbook 1"
Illustrations: Mgr. Kateřina Kovářová
Translation, adaptation, and graphic design: Roman Placzek, D.M.A.
Publisher: BumbleBeeNotes™ Music Publishing, Manlius, NY, USA, 2024
Catalog number: cbbn002-wb-003
Website: www.bumblebeenotes.com
Copyright: BumbleBee Notes™ Inc. Music Corporation
ISBN: 979-8-9919035-2-3

What's Inside:

Musical staff
Notes and rests
Treble clef
Measures and time signatures
Note and rest values
Notes on the musical staff

My dear musical friends,

While we were learning and making music in my first book, Clefi's Little Notebook, many of you asked for additional fun activities, quizzes, and coloring tasks to help you practice everything we learned together. Therefore, I have prepared a little surprise for you: three music workbooks filled with all those activities! You are holding the first of them, Clefi's Music Workbook 1, where you can practice drawing the treble clef, understanding the duration of notes and rests, and recognizing time signatures. We will focus on feeling the tempo of the music, identifying note values, and playing with the rhythm of songs. So, let's get started! I am excited for our musical time together!

Yours, Clefi

Similar to "Clefi's Little Notebook," this book presents a collection of enchanting folk songs from the rich Czech folklore tradition, designed for music education. To accurately utilize their intended purpose, each song requires accurate adaptation and translation into English, which would take up more space than these volumes can accommodate without disrupting their intended design. Therefore, we are offering a standalone "Clefi & Notelina's Songbook," featuring all the songs from all nine volumes of Clefi's New Music Education School series, along with accurately and sensibly translated and adapted English lyrics.

Musical Staff

Clefi's Little Notebook, pg. 18 and 19

The musical staff has **five lines** and **four spaces.**

E Trace the **entire lines** of the musical staff: the **first** line **green**, the **second** line **yellow**, the **third line red**, the **fourth line purple**, and the **fifth** line **blue.**

E Color the **entire spaces** of the musical staff: the **first space brown**, the **second** space **green**, the **third space orange**, and the **fourth** space **blue.**

Note

The **note** is a **musical symbol** for the **tone**.
The notes live on the **musical staff**.

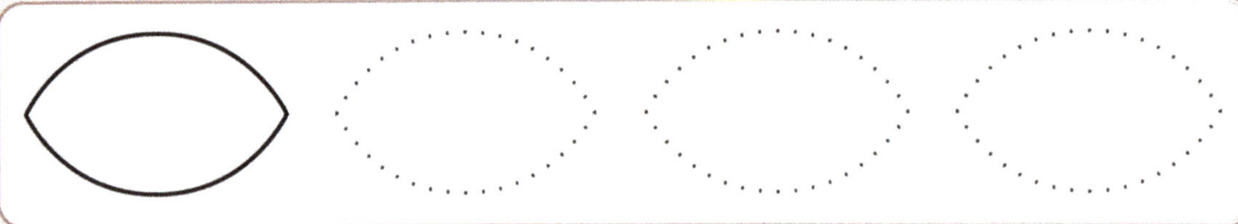

On the **musical staff**, notes can be placed
at **one** of **two places**:

on a line - 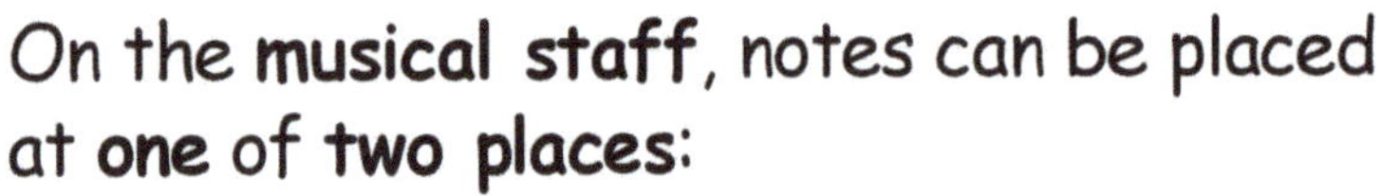

in a space - 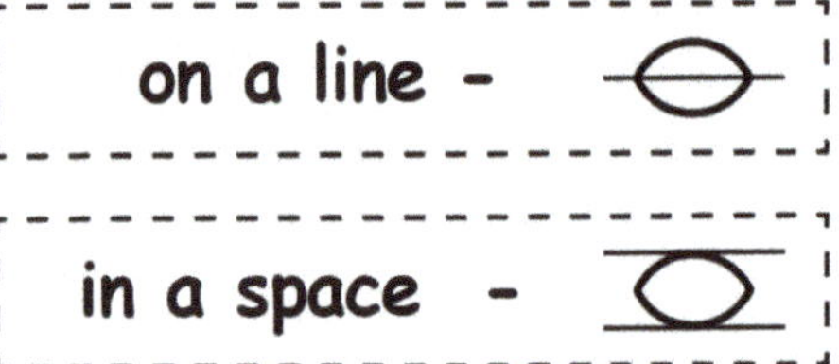

E Color the **kite's bows**.
Use **yellow** for bows with **notes** on a **line**
and **red** for those with **notes** in a **space**.

E Practice drawing **notes** on a **line**.

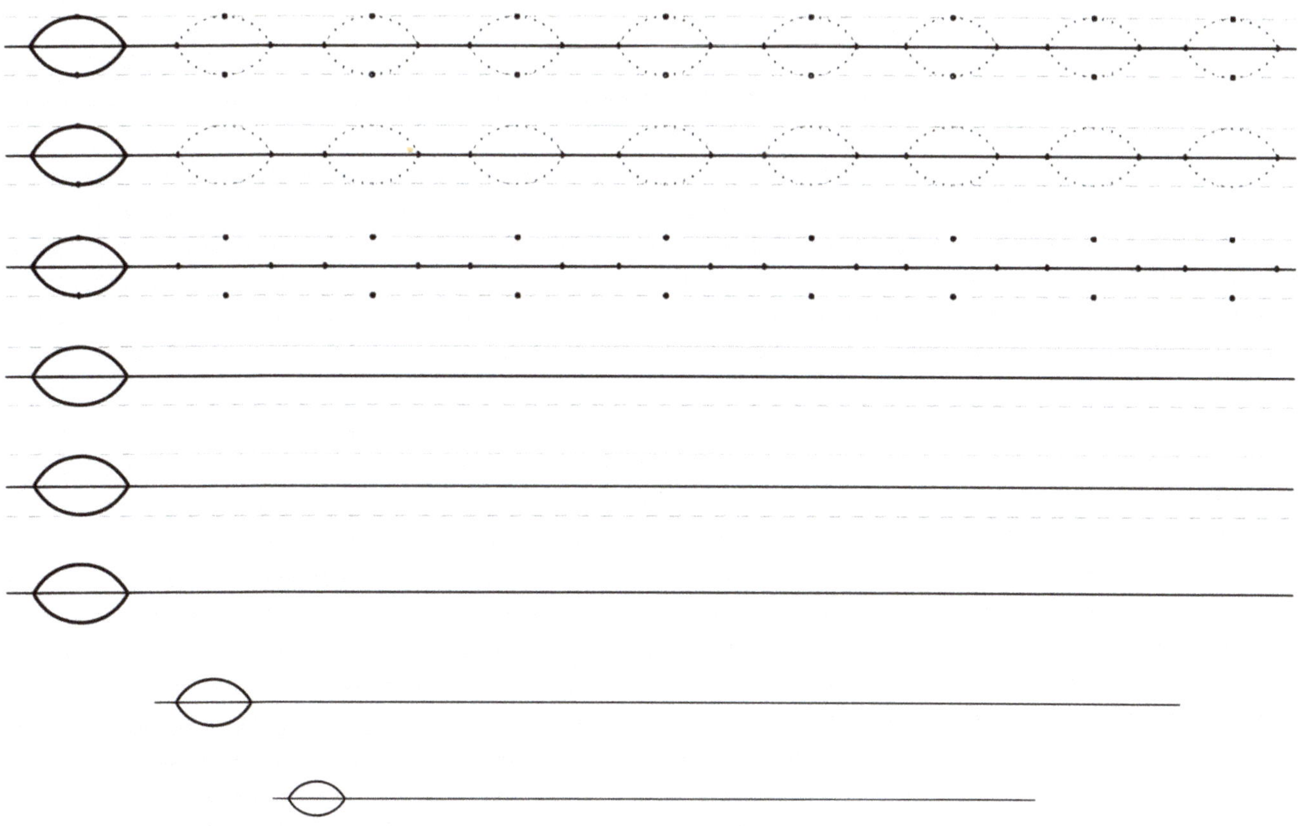

E Practice drawing **notes** in a **space**.

Treble Clef

Clefi's Little Notebook, pg. 22 and 23

The **treble** or violin clef is known as **the G clef.** It encircles the second staff line, which is home to **the note G4.**

Clefi drew a few treble clefs. Cross out the **incorrect** ones.

Which of the following **treble clefs** starts on the **correct line**? Circle the **correct** treble clefs in **green**. In all examples, **highlight** the line where the treble clef **should** begin in **red**.

Measure & Time Signature
Clefi's Little Notebook, pg. 30 and 31

Measures are small compartments on the **musical staff** where we write the **notes**. When we clap steady without any change in pace while singing a song, we are clapping the **beats**.

Songs have **short** and **long beats**. • short — long

E Mark the beats of the first two measures of the songs using dots and dashes. Count **four beats** per measure: **one-two-three-four**.

one	two	three	four	one	two	three	four	
•	•	•	•	—		—		***Cat Hid Under a Fence*** *Clefi's Little Notebook, pg. 53*
								Rain is Falling *Clefi's Little Notebook, pg. 55*
								Cat is Coming Down *Clefi's Little Notebook, pg. 54*
								Little Vixen, Run! *Clefi's Little Notebook, pg. 54*
								Our Fence Fell Down *Clefi's Little Notebook, pg. 57*

measure measure

E Mark the beats of the first two measures of the songs using dots and dashes. These songs, we count in **three**: **one-two-three**.

one	two	three	one	two	three	
•	•	•	—		•	***Run, Run, Run, Katy,*** *Clefi's Little Notebook, pg. 57*
						On the Tree, Our Pear Tree *Clefi's Little Notebook, pg. 52*
						Hey-Ho, Little Sheep *Clefi's Little Notebook, pg. 56*
						Go to Sleep, My Little Starlight *Clefi's Little Notebook, pg. 52*
						Mail is Coming *Clefi & Notelina's Songbook, pg. 44*

measure

The time signature belongs at the **beginning** of the **staff**, just after the clef. It tells us **how we count** the **beats** within each measure.

The **four-four** measure has **four beats**. We mark it with numbers **4/4** or the letter **C**.

The **numbers** are **stacked** in the **center** of the staff.

The letter **C** is **placed** between the **second** and **fourth lines**.

The **three-four** measure has **three beats**. We mark it with numbers **3/4**.

Notes & Rests

Clefi's Little Notebook, pg. 24 - 29

A **note** is a musical symbol for a specific **tone**.
The **note's shape** tells us the **note's duration**.

The notes with empty heads are longer: 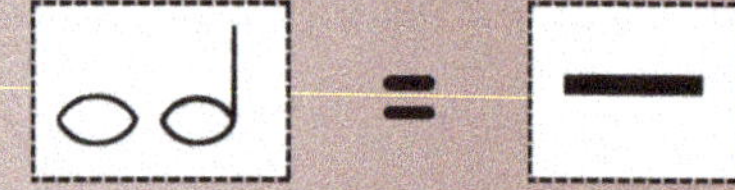

The notes with filled heads are shorter: 

E Color the train cars with **longer** heads **yellow** and those with the **short** ones **blue**.

A **rest** is a musical symbol for **silence in music**.
Its **shape** tells us the **rest's duration**.

Longer rests sit on or hang from a line: 

The shorter rests have a vertical shape: 

E Color the mushrooms with longer rests **brown** and those with the **short** ones **red**.

Mark the notes' duration of the song's section with dots and dashes. Leave the squares with rests **empty**. Count **four beats** per measure.

one   two three four   one   two three four

Cows Are Coming Down
Clefi & Notelina's Songbook, pg. 30

Silly Dog Jumped Like a Frog
Clefi's Little Notebook, pg. 53

I am a Little Gees Herding Girl
Clefi & Notelina's Songbook, pg. 31

Little Sheep, Not a Peep!
Clefi's Little Notebook, pg. 51

Do you recognize the songs in the pictures? They are from Clefi's Songbook in *Clefi's Little Notebook*. Color the balloons with songs in **4/4 meter yellow** and the ones with the songs in **3/4 meter green**.

See Clefi's Little Notebook, pg. 31 and 32

Color the pictures!

Whole Note
Clefi's Little Notebook, pg. 26

The **whole note** has **four beats**.
It is basically just an **empty notehead**.

E Draw **whole notes** on a staff **line**.

E Draw **whole notes** in a staff **space**.

Notes on Musical Staff

Clefi's Little Notebook, pg. 20

When writing them on the **musical staff**, the **notes** can be placed on the
lines and **spaces**, on the **top** and right **below** the **staff**,
and on the **ledger lines**.

E Draw **notes** on the **lines** according to their **numbers**.

E Draw **notes** in the **spaces** according to their **numbers**.

E Circle the **notes** on the **top of the staff** in **red** and the ones **below** in **blue**.

E Trace the **ledger lines** and draw **notes on them**.

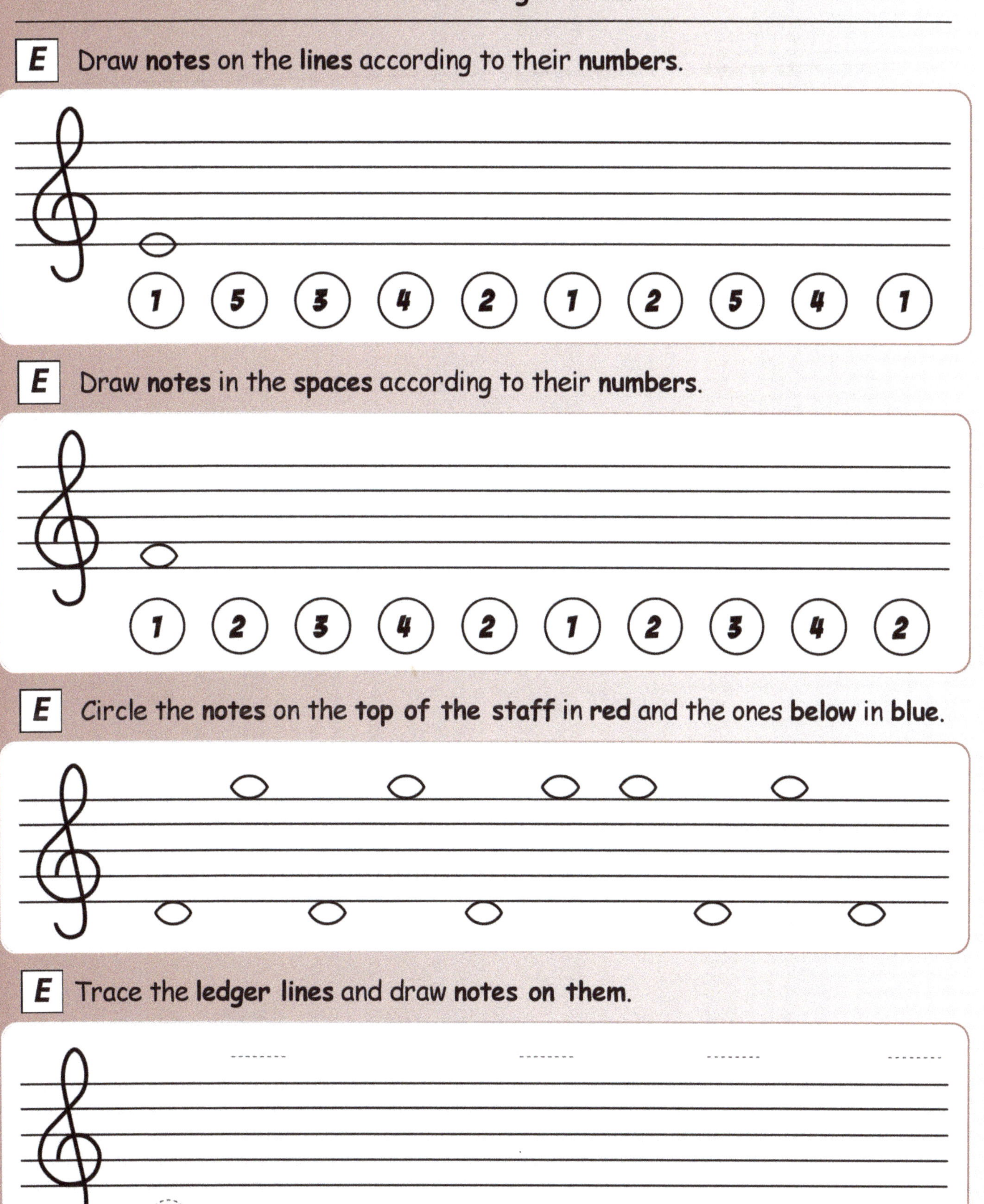

Half Note

Clefi's Little Notebook, pg. 26

The **half note** has **two beats**.
It has an **empty head** and a **stem**.

E Draw **half notes** on a staff **line**.

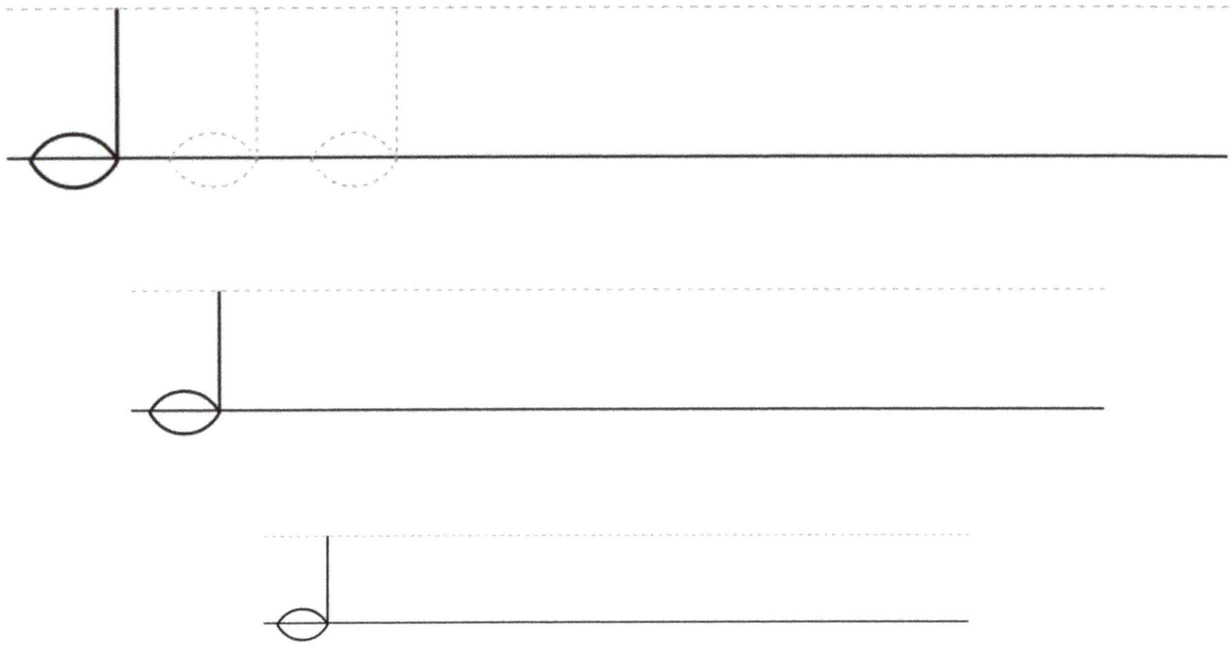

E Draw **half notes** in a staff **space**.

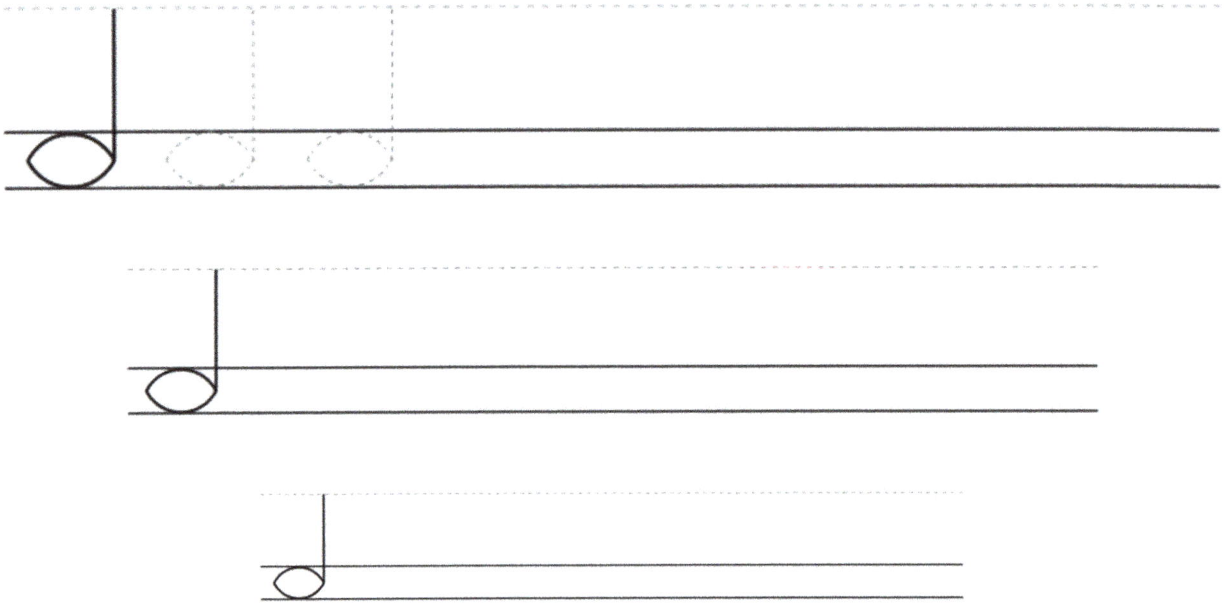

Note Stem

Clefi's Little Notebook, pg. 24, 25, and 28

The **stem** is connected to a note on the **right side upward**
or on the **left side downward.**

on the **left** side **downwards**

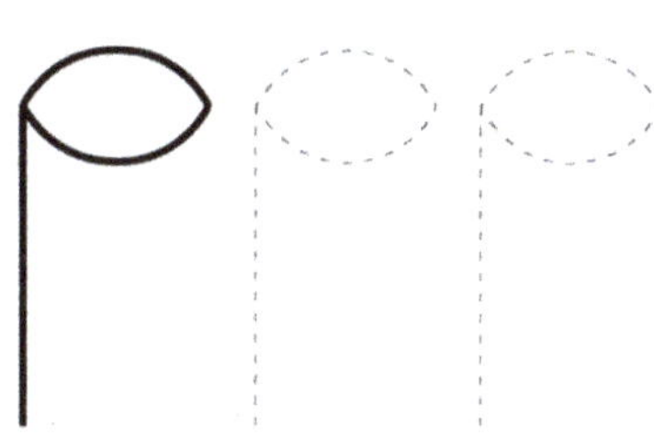

on the **right** side **upwards**

E Practice drawing **half notes** with **stems** in **both** directions.

Notes With Stem on Staff

Clefi's Little Notebook, pg. 27 and 28

Notes placed in the **lower section** of the **musical staff** have their **stems** on the **right side upward**. Notes in the **upper section** are written with their **stems** on the **left side downward**.

E Practice the **stem placement** and **direction** by tracing the notes.

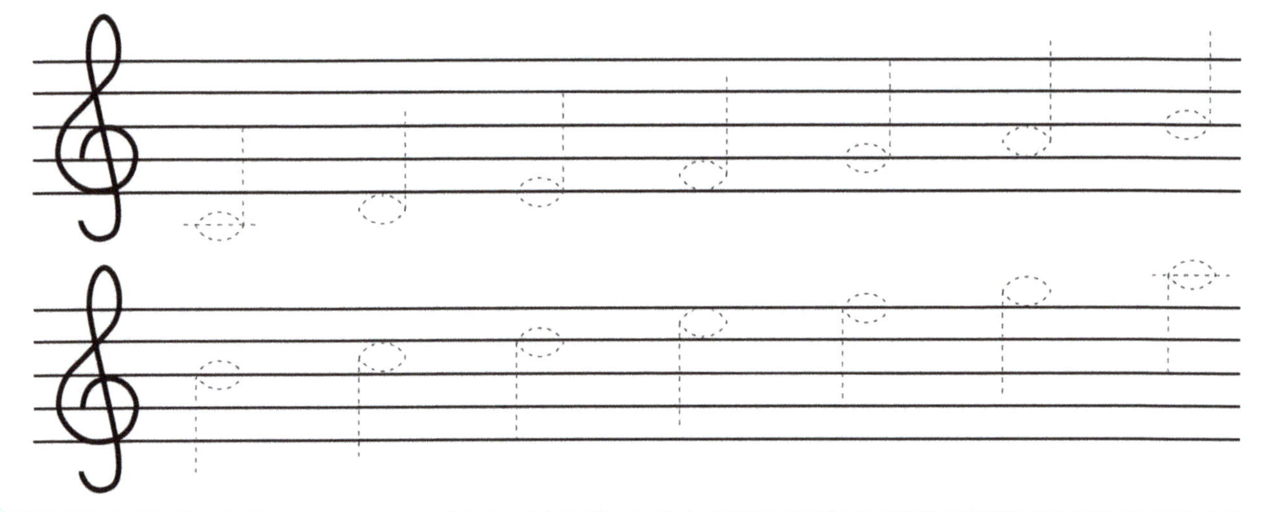

E Complete the **half notes** with the **correctly** placed and directed **stems**.

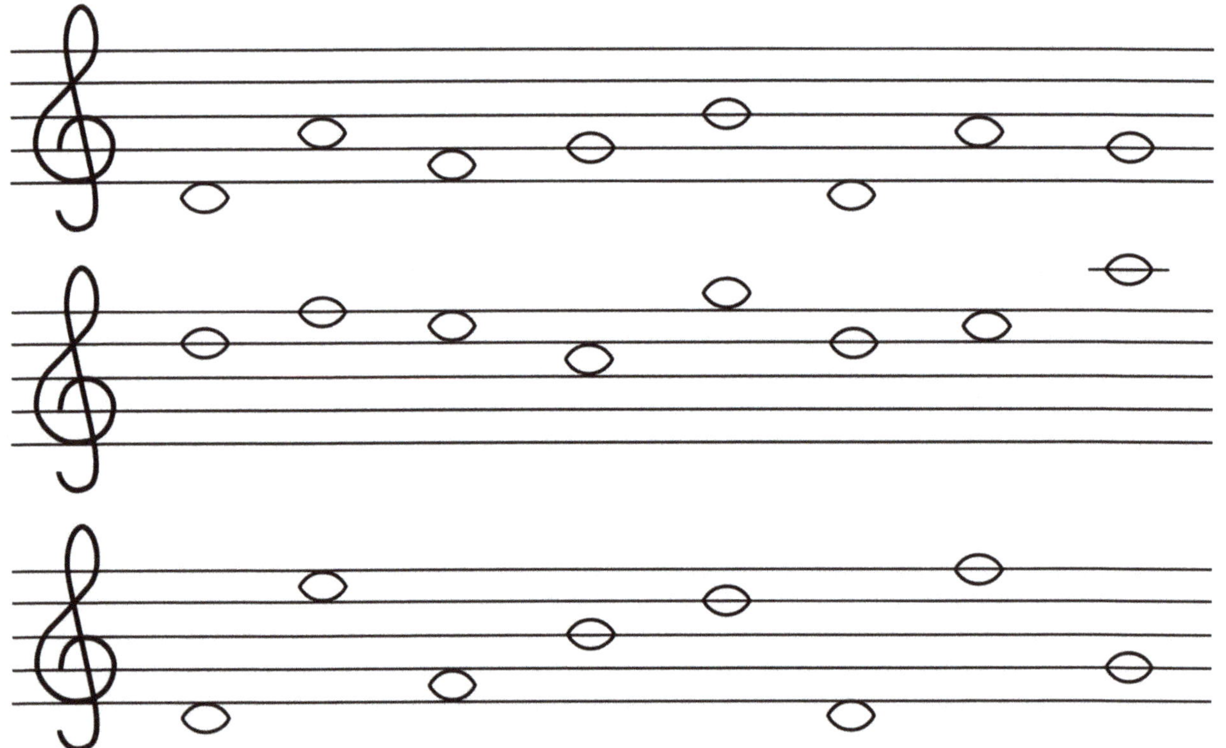

Color ONLY the flowers with the notes that have correctly placed stems.

Circle the correctly written notes in green.

Complete the half notes by adding correct stems.

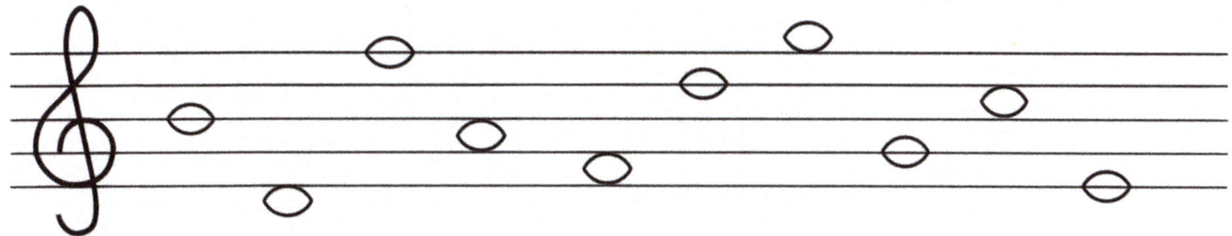

Whole and Half Notes

Clefi's Little Notebook, pg. 26

E Color the apples with **whole notes red** and the ones with **half notes yellow**.

E Help Clefi get **home** to find out **what note** awaits him.

Color the Celfi!

Connect **pictures** that **belong** together. All you need to remember is how many **beats** a **whole note** have and how many a **half note**.

Draw **notes** into the **flower heads**. The **number** on the **flower pots** tell you if a **whole note** or a **half note**.

Whole Rest

Clefi's Little Notebook, pg. 29

The **whole rest** has **four beats.**
It **hangs down** from the **fourth line**

E Trace the **fourth lines** in **green**, then fill the staffs with **whole rests.**

Half Rest

The **half rest** has **two beats.**
It **sits** on the **third line**

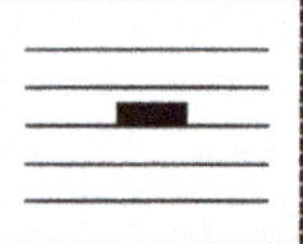

E Trace the **third lines** in **blue**, then fill the staffs with **half rests.**

Whole and Half Rests

 Fill in the **rests** according to the **number** of **beats** below the staff.

 What rests lives in each house? Write the **number** of the **beats** on the roof. Color the houses with **whole** rests **green** and the ones with **half** rests **orange**.

Little Review

 On the **right** boot, write the **number** of beats of the **rest** on the **left** boot.

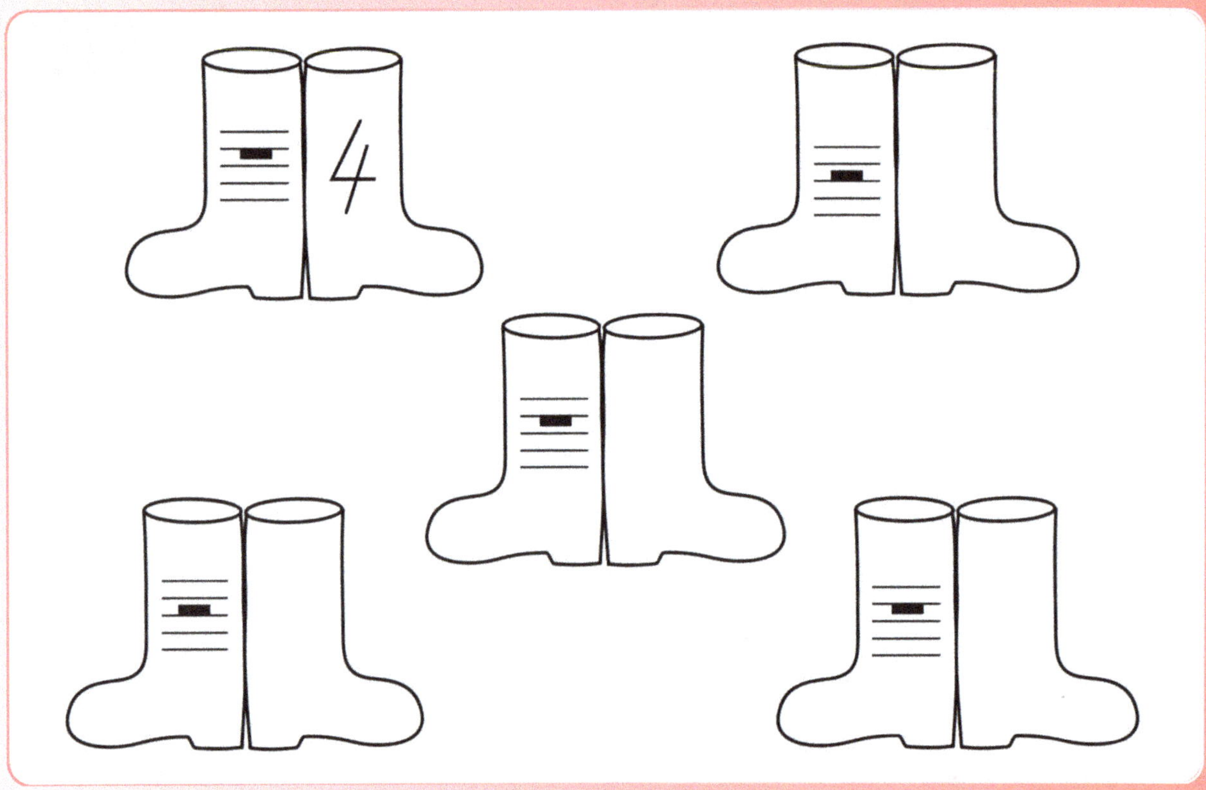

 Link each **note** and **rest** with their matching numbers.
Don't forget to use **colorful crayons**!

E Color the picture. Pick a **different color** for every **section**, BUT ensure you use the **same** color for the **sections** with the **notes** and **rests** of the **same value**.

Solve the **musical math problems** by filling in the **notes** and **rests** with the correct number of beats in the **empty squares** of the **corresponding tables**.

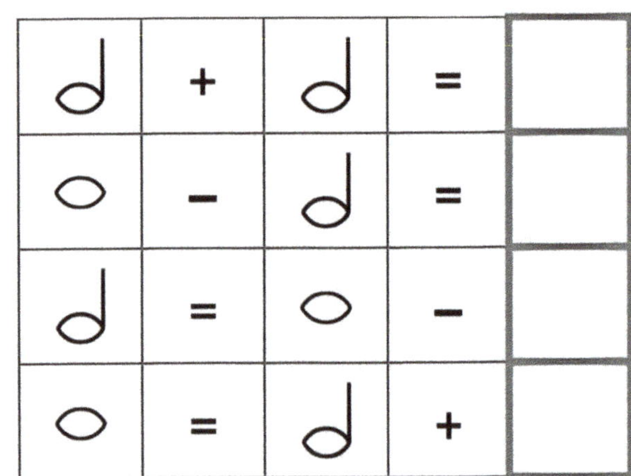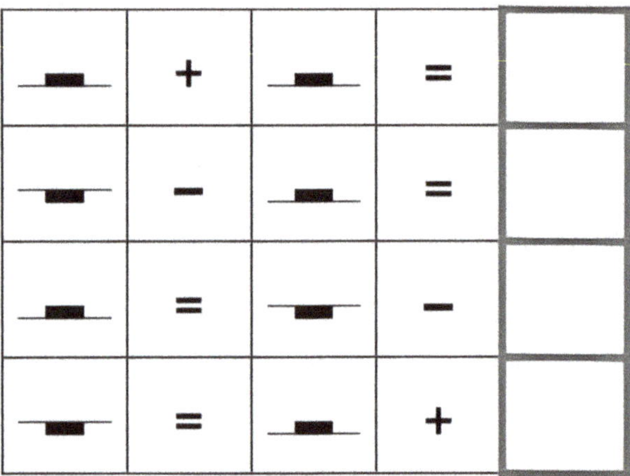

Can you see the **measures** with **missing notes** and **rests**? **Without** mixing them up, complete the measures with **notes** and **rests** to ensure the **correct number** of beats in each **measure**.

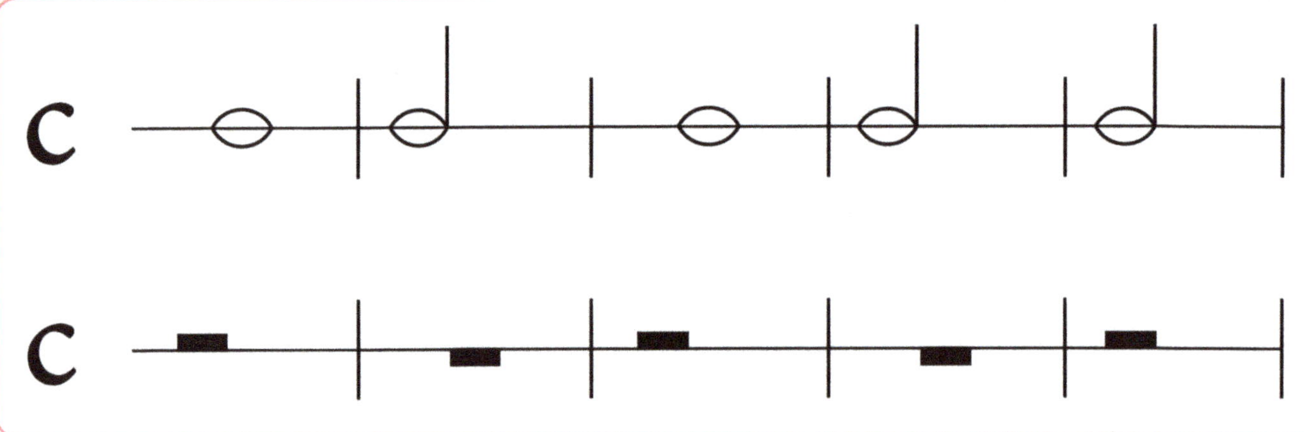

Fill in whatever **musical symbol** for a **tone** or **silence** to ensure the **correct number** of beats in every measure.

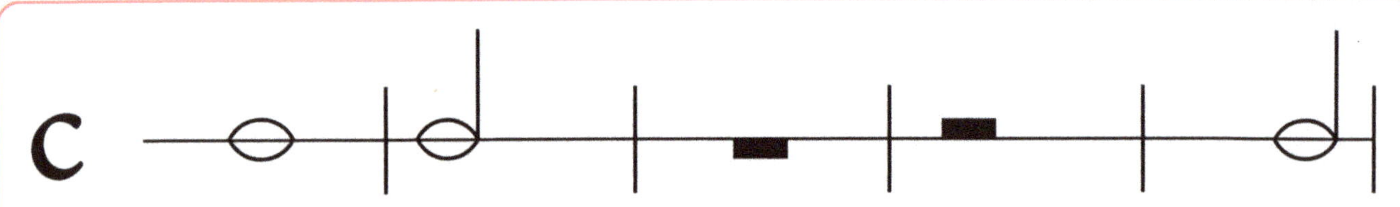

Do you recognize the songs from the pictures below? You can find them all in *Clefi's Songbook* at the end of *Clefi's Little Notebook* (page 51). Connect the **correct meter bubbles** with the **song bubbles**. And color the pictures!

Quarter Note
Clefi's Little Notebook, pg. 26

The **quarter note** has **one beat**.
It has a **filled head** and a **stem**.

E Practice drawing the **quarter notes**.

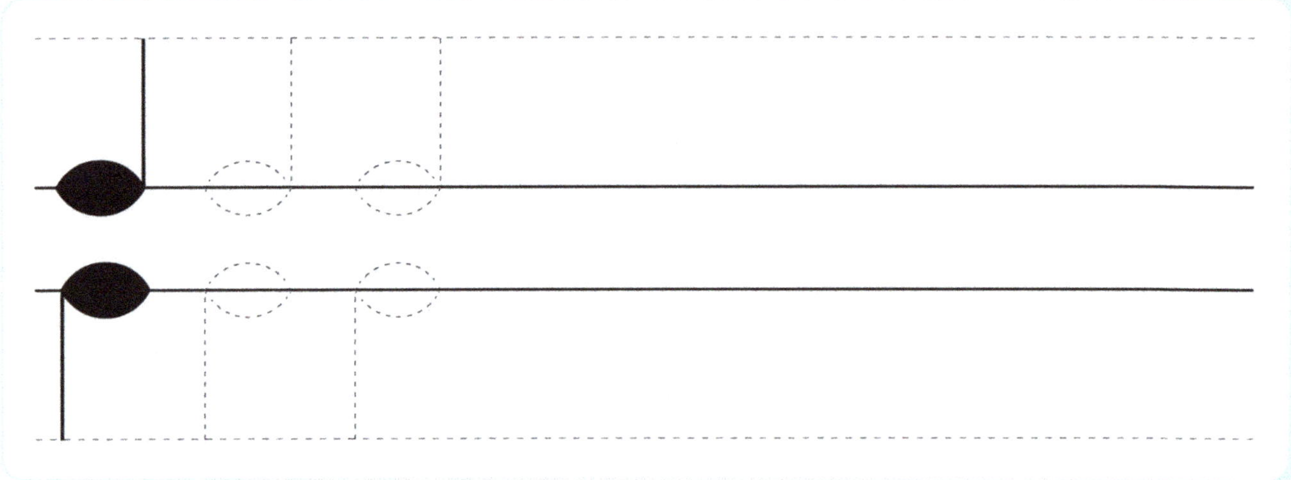

E Do you remember the rule of **stem placement** and **direction**? Complete the **quarter notes** with the **correct stems**.

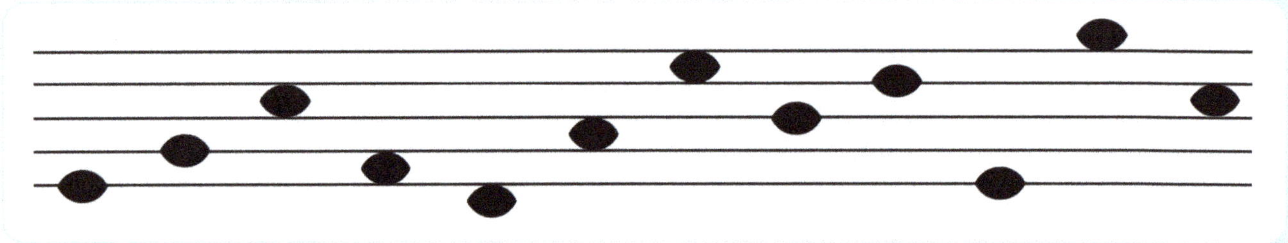

E How many beats does a **quarter note** have, and **how many does** a **half note** have? Fill in the **heads** of the **quarter notes** based on the **number** of **beats** shown in the **squares** above the notes.

| 1 | 2 | 1 | 1 | 2 | 2 | 1 | 2 | 1 | 2 |

E Write the **number** of **beats** for every **note** into the square next to it.

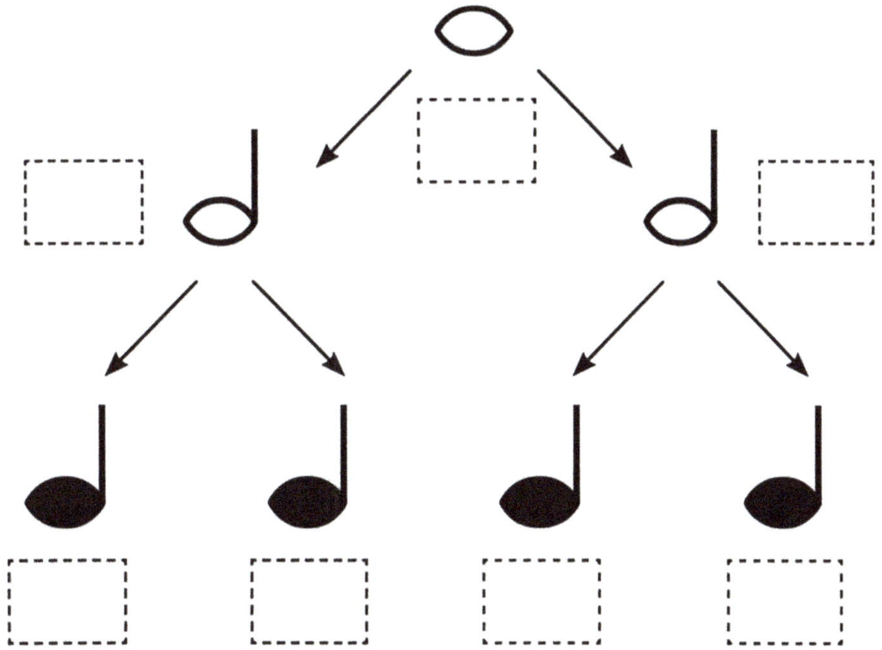

E Fill the tables according to the example.

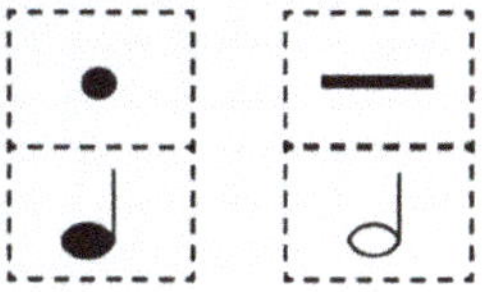

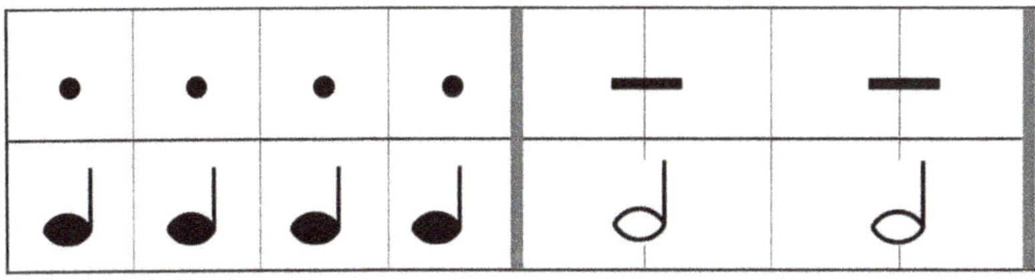

Cat is Coming Down
Clefi's Little Notebook, pg. 54

Little Vixen, Run!
Clefi's Little Notebook, pg. 54

Mean Bagpiper
Clefi's Little Notebook, pg. 55

**Go to Sleep,
My Little Starlight**
Clefi's Little Notebook, pg. 52

Quarter Rest

Clefi's Little Notebook, pg. 29

The **quarter rest** has **one beat**. It looks like a **lightning bolt** and sits in the **middle** of the **staff**.

Let's learn to draw the **quarter rest**.

1. First, **draw** an **arrowhead** pointing to the right on the fourth line.

2. Then, **cross** the **middle line** down to the right.

3. The last step is a **nice bend across** the **second line**.

E Practice drawing the **quarter rest**.

E **Find** all circles with **quarter notes** and **quarter rests** and **color them in.** Did you find the **hidden image**?

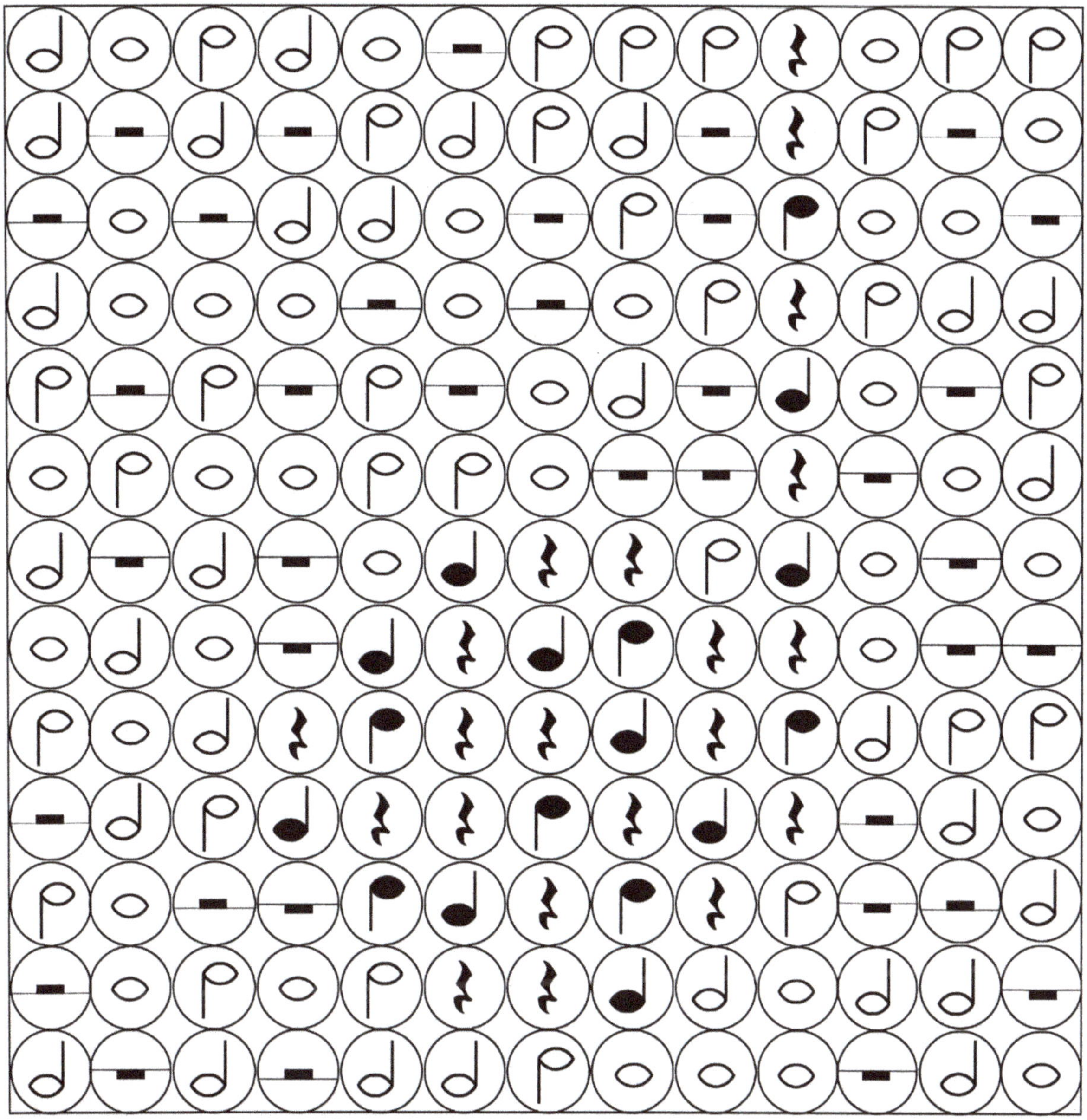

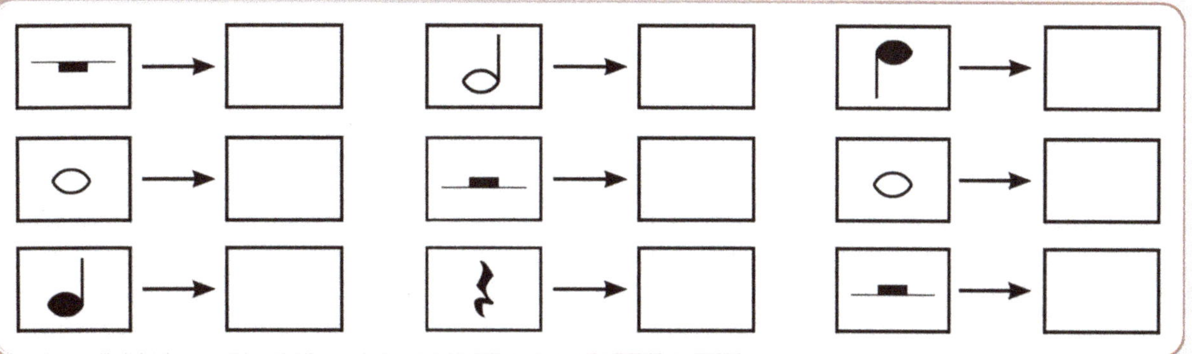

E Write the **number** of **beats** into the squares next to the **musical symbols**.

Eighth Note

Clefi's Little Notebook, pg. 26

The **eighth note** is **half** a **beat** long. It features a **filled notehead**, a **stem**, and a **flag** or **beam** when **linked** with other **eighth notes**.

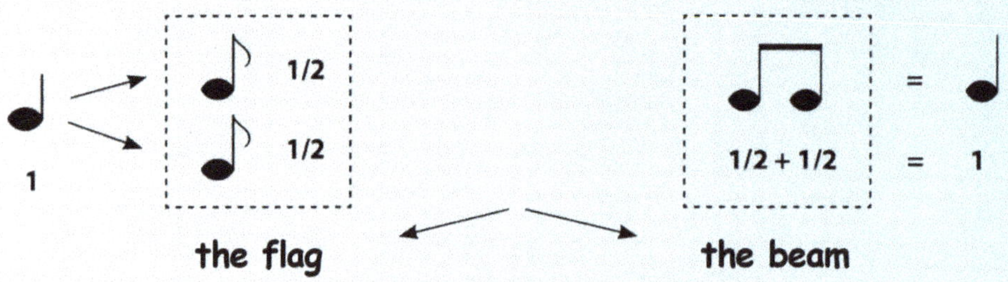

E Practice drawing **eighth notes**, **flags**, and **beams**.

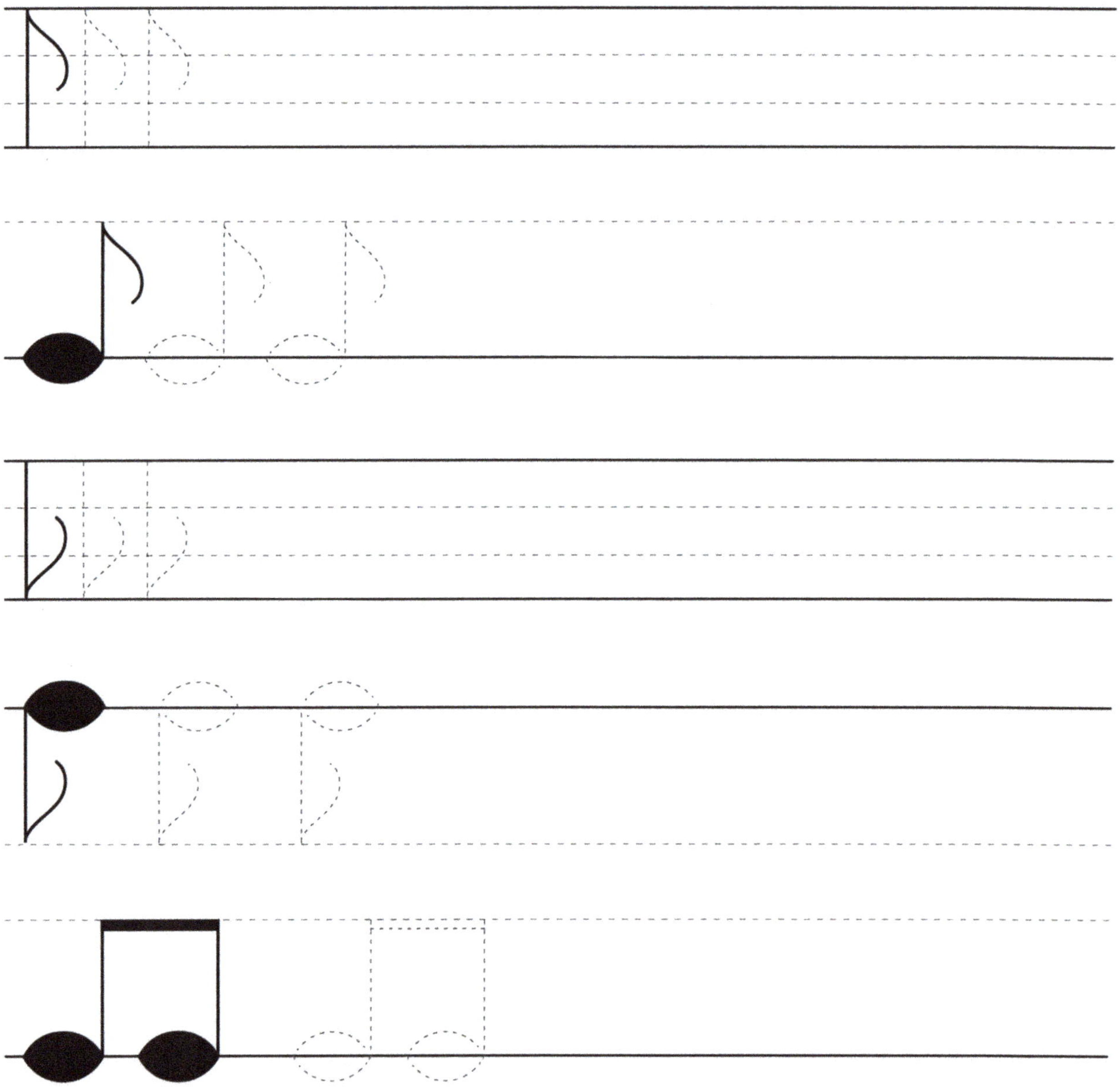

Eighth Rest

Clefi's Little Notebook, pg. 29

The **eighth rest** is **half** of the **beat long**. It looks like a **funny candy cane** and sits in the **middle** of the **staff**.

Drawing an **eighth rest** is quite simple. Begin with a **little dot** and a **gentle downward curve** on the **fourth line**, then add the **leg downward** to the **left** to the second line.

E Connect each **flower** with its **corresponding flower pot**. Pay attention to the **symbols** and the **number of beats**!

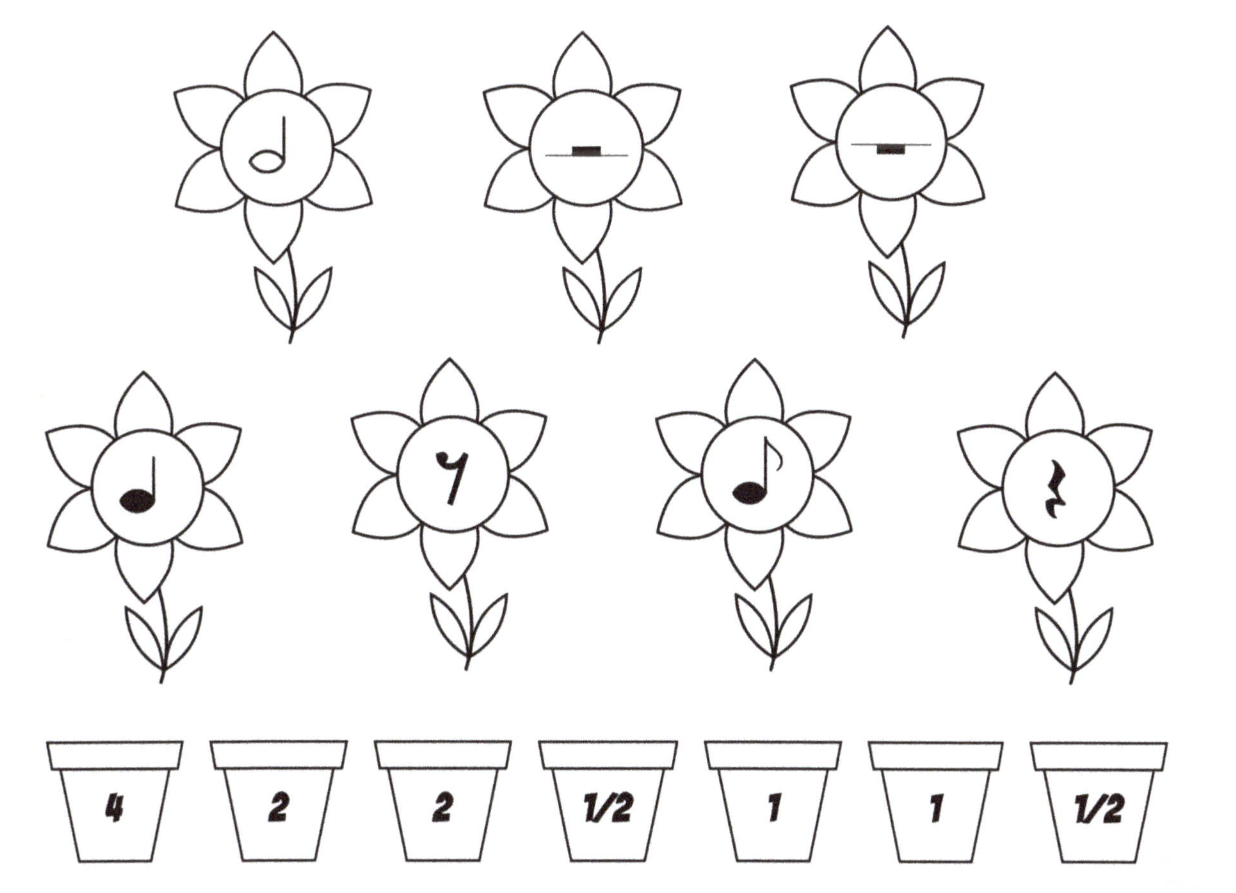

Big Review

 Solve the **musical math problems** and connect each **letter** with the **stamp** with the **correct beat postage**.

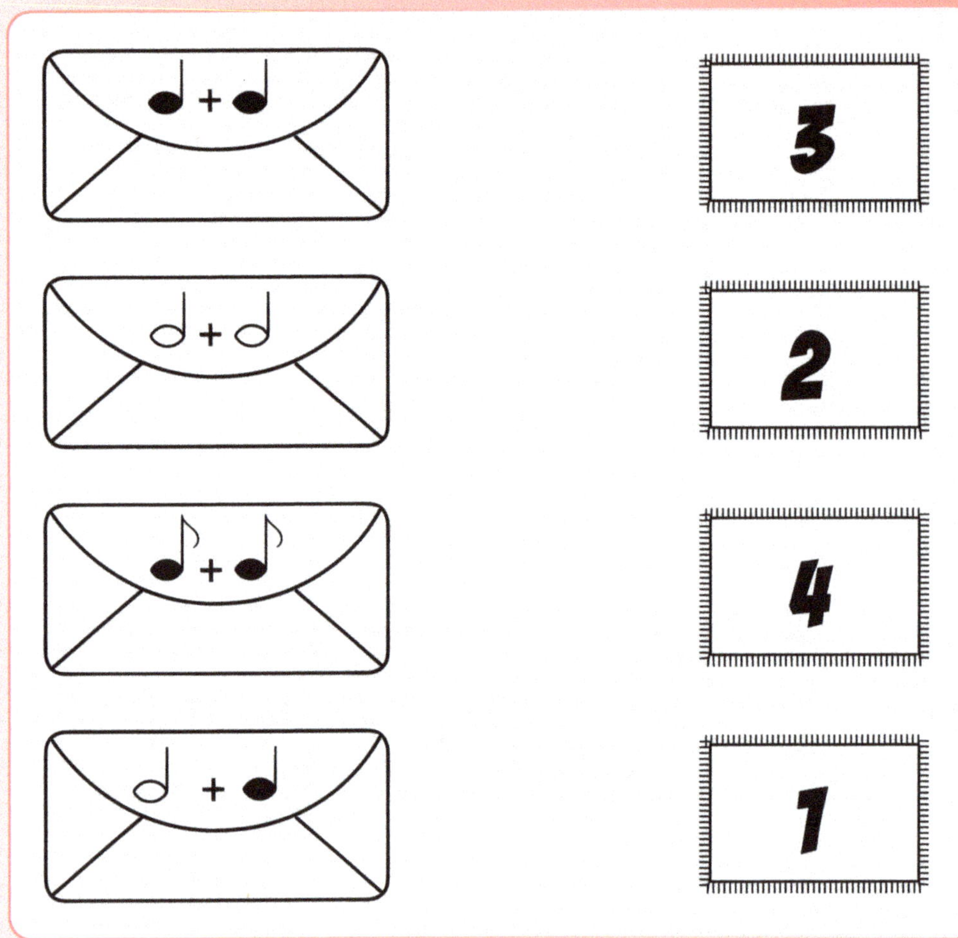

 Connect the **stamps** with the **same beat value**.

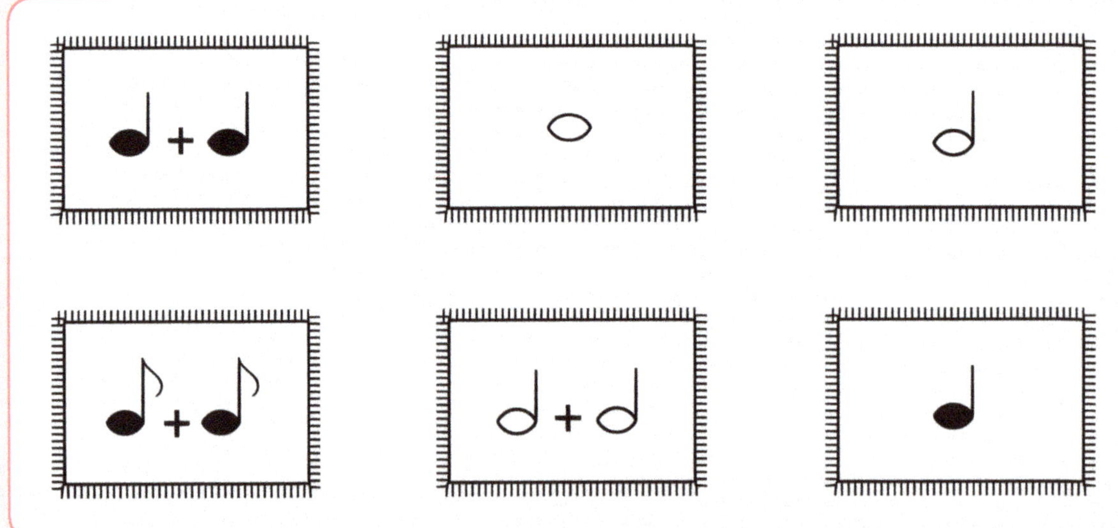

Draw the **treble clef** at the beginning of the **staff**, then complete the **half notes** by adding **correctly placed stems**.

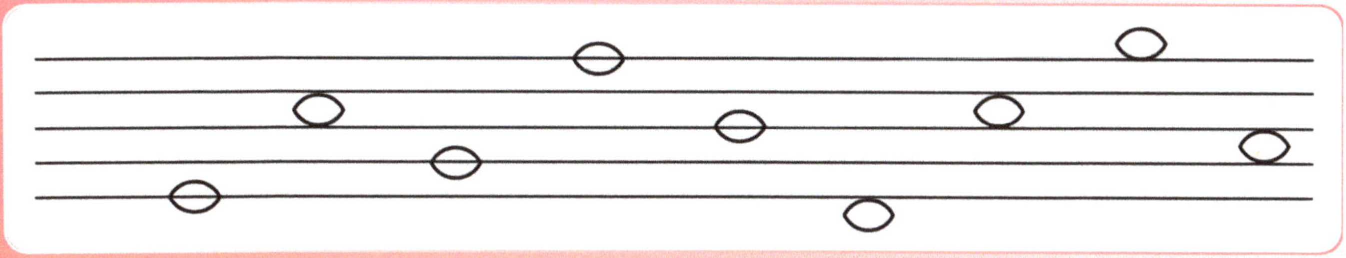

Complete the **notes** so their **value corresponds** with the **number** of the **beats** indicated below them. Connect two neighboring **eighth notes** with a **beam**.

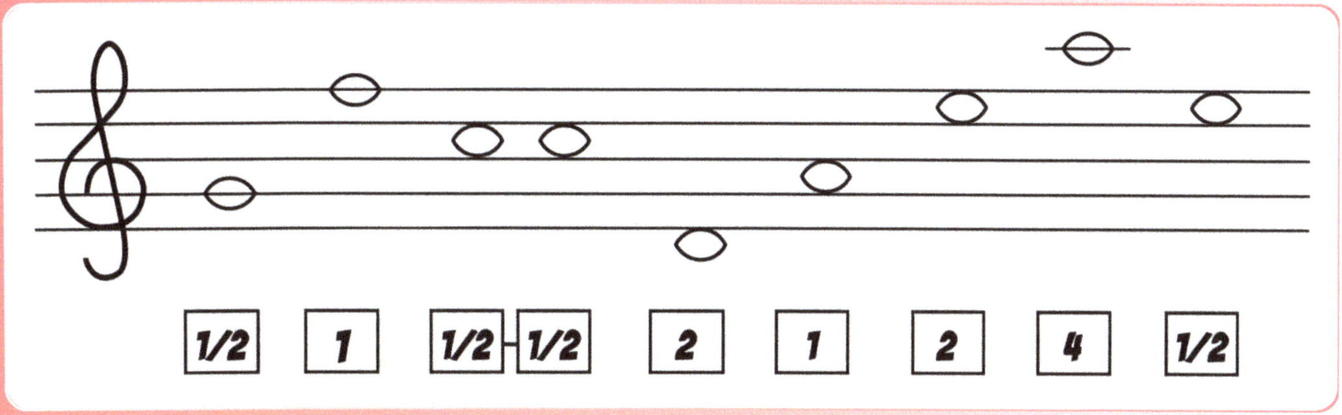

Write the **number** of **beats** of each **note** and **rest** into the squares below them.

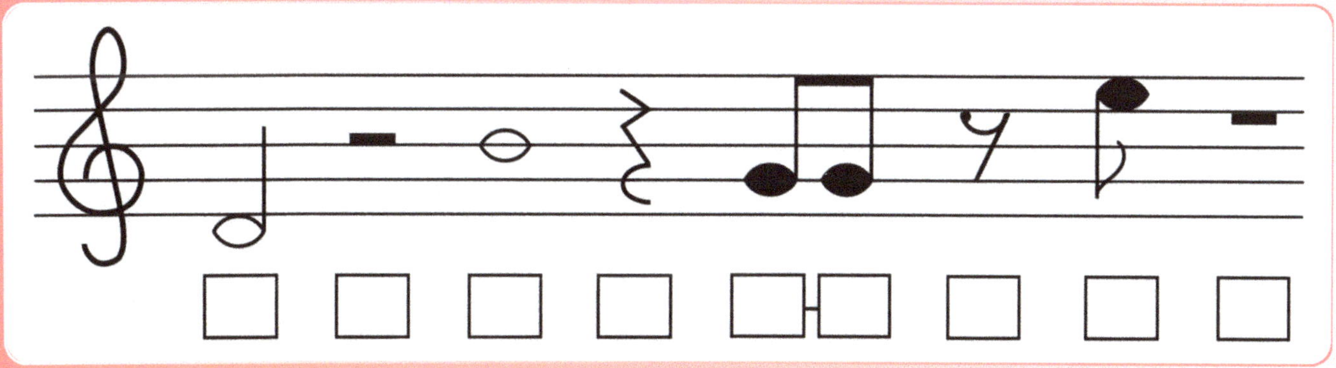

Draw the **note** that represents the **result** of the **musical math problem**. Write the **number** of **beats** for each note into the squares below them.

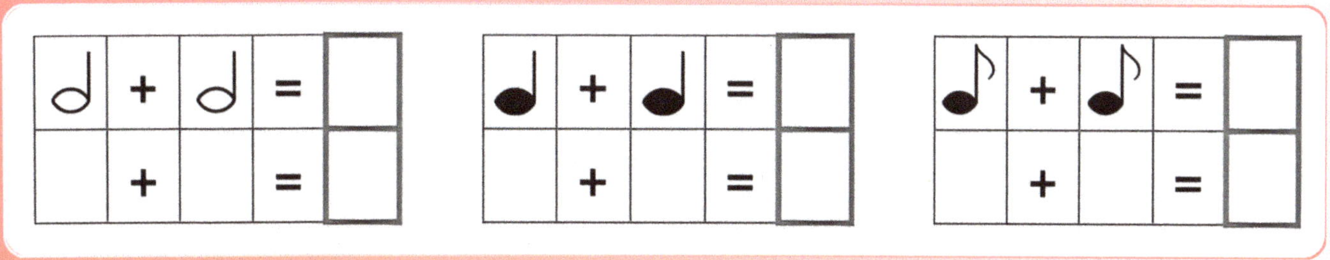

 Fill in the empty slots with the **correct number** of beats. Then, draw the **treble clef** and the **correct time signature** (meter) on the staffs.

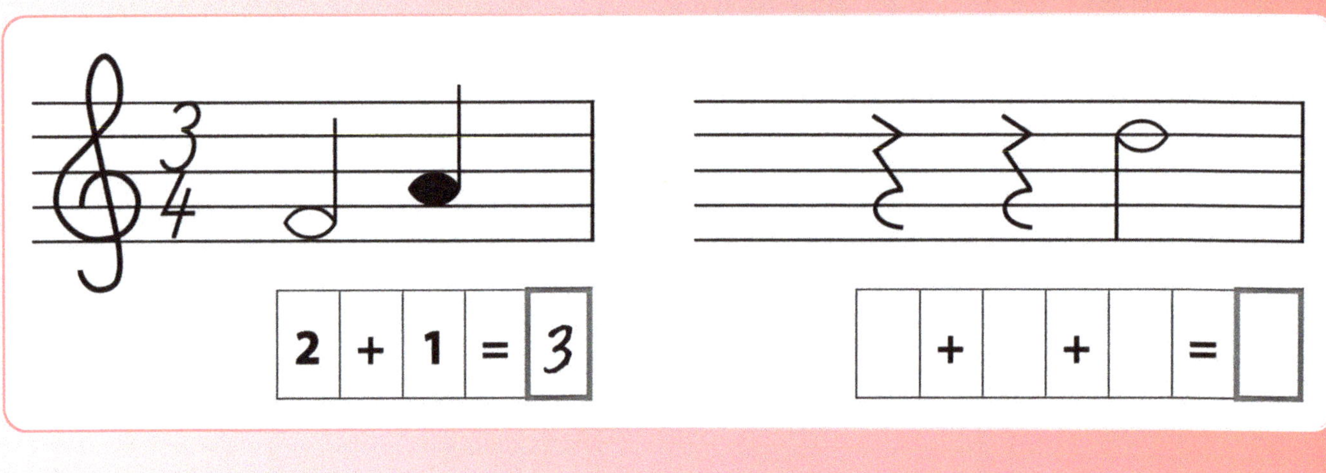

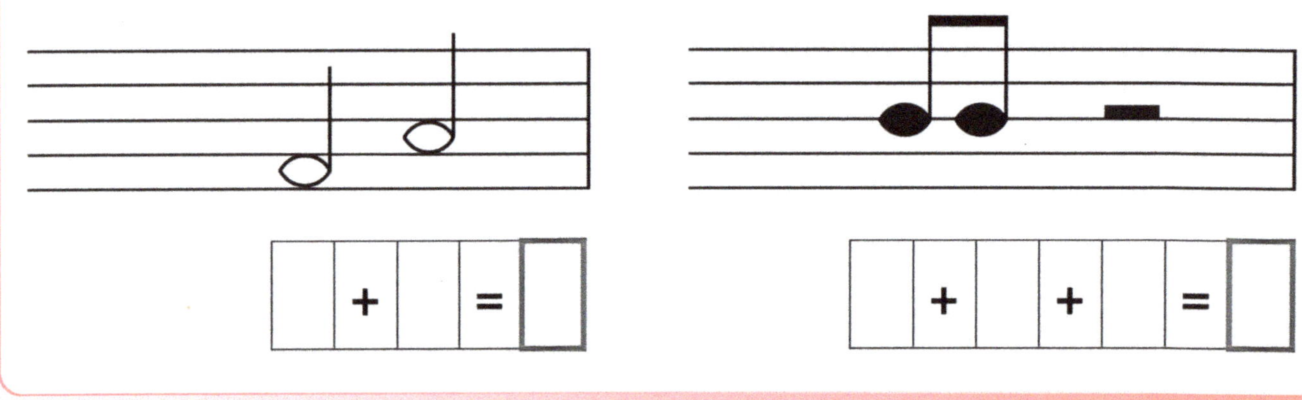

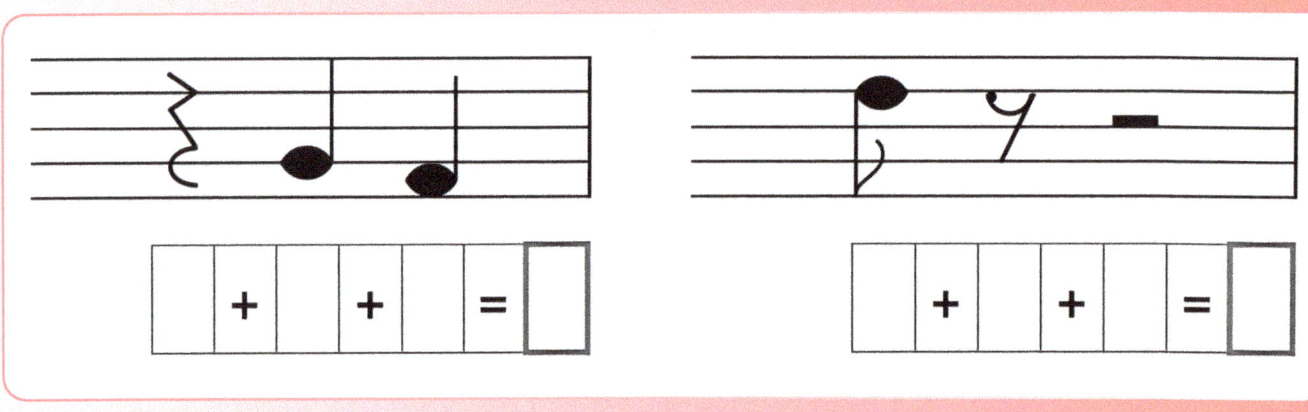

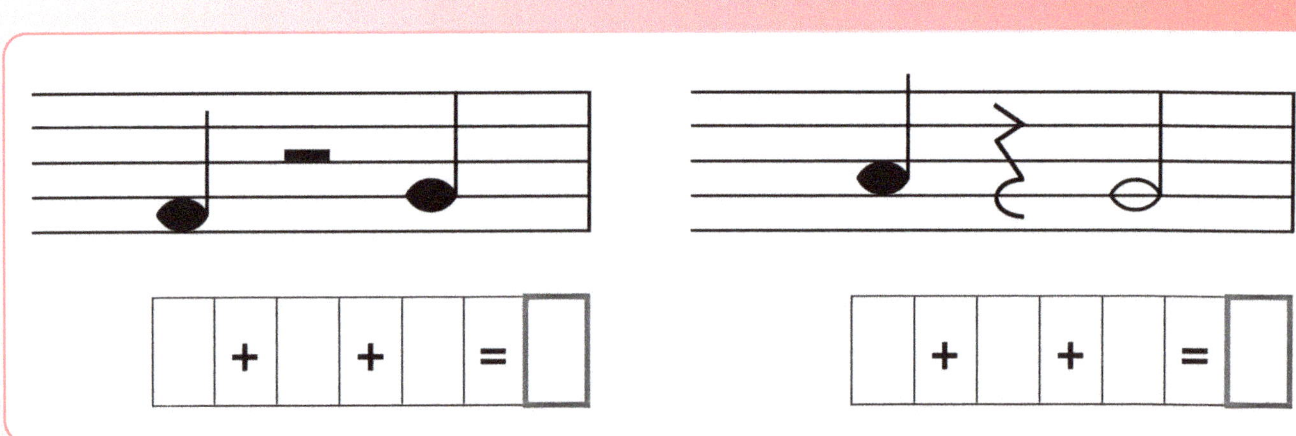

CERTIFICATE

OF COMPLETION

This certificate is presented to:

____

For successfully completing

Clefi's Music Workbook 1

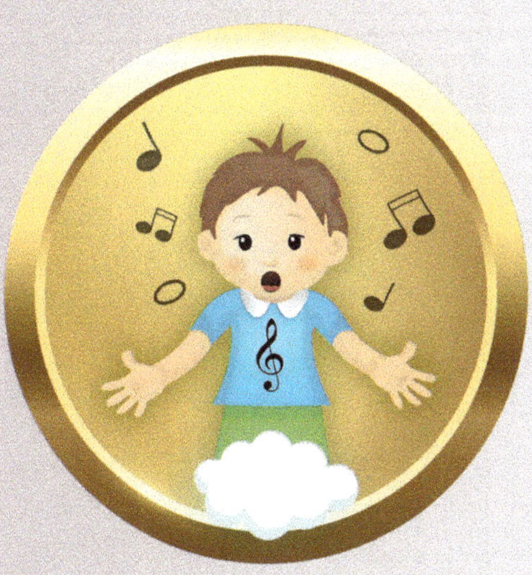

____

music education teacher

Clefi's Little American-British Music Dictionary

Note & Rest Values

Whole note .... Semibreve

Whole rest .... Semibreve pause

Half note .... Minim

Half rest .... Minim pause

Quarter note .... Crotchet

Quarter rest .... Crotchet pause

Eighth note .... Quaver

Eight rest .... Quaver pause

Note Distances

Whole step .... Tone

Half step .... Semitone

Octaves

Fourth octave .... One-line octave

Fifth octave .... Two-line octave

Notes

C4-B4 .... c'-b' (one-line c-b)

C5 .... c'' (two-line c)